Contents

Poems about bullying

Why won't they talk to me?

Why won't they talk to me?

Each day it's just the same.

No one will talk to me.

To them it's like a game.

When I walk into the room,

they turn their heads away.

No one will sit by me.

No one asks me to play.

What have I done to them?

Why do they pick on me?

What am I doing wrong?

Please someone, talk to me.

John Foster

Names

I don't like them and what they say.

They laugh at me and run away.

Just because I'm not the same,

I'm not asked to join their games.

The names they call me hurt, they know,

a lot more than the hardest blow.

When I hear those names, I cry

and feel as if I want to die.

Marian Swinger

Ways

They do not have to touch you

to make you feel like dirt.

They have more clever ways to do it,

when they want to hurt.

They do not even have to use

a word, a noise, a name.

The ways they have are much more quiet,

but hurt you all the same.

It only takes a kind of look

to make you really sad.

Or acting like you are not there,

which can be just as bad.

Tony Mitton

It hurts

It hurts when people call you names.

It hurts when they point and grin.

It hurts when they say things about

the colour of your skin.

It hurts when people laugh at you,

because you cover your hair.

It hurts when they make fun of you,

because of what you wear.

It hurts when people say to you,

'We don't like you living here.'

We haven't done anything to them.

What is it that they fear?

John Foster

Play safe

'Morning, Jack,' I say.

'Have I said you could speak?' shouts Jack.

'No.'

'Have I said you could say "no"?'

'No.'

'You talk when I say you can. Understand?'

'Yes.'

'Did I say you could say "yes"?'

I want to shout,

'Leave me alone!'

But I hear a voice in my head say,

'Play safe. Keep your mouth shut.'

John Coldwell

If you tell

'If you tell, we'll get you.'

That's what they always say.

So I give them what they want.

It's easier that way.

They take my things.

They break my things.

They know I'll never tell.

For telling tales just isn't done.

But not telling tales is hell.

John Foster

They used to pick on Angela

They used to pick on Angela.

'She asks for it!' they said:

'The way she sticks her lip out!'

'The way she hangs her head!'

'The way she cannot catch a ball!'

'The way she goes all red!'

Angela has left now, so

they pick on me instead,

I know I never asked for it,

I wish they'd all drop dead.

But I will NOT put up with it:

I'm going to tell the Head.

Celia Warren

Bully

Why, each day,

do you stop and stare,

do you chant those names,

do you pull my hair?

Why, each day,

have you never tried

to know the hurt

that I feel inside?

Andrew Collett

I was bullied once

I was bullied once.

Now I'm a bully too.

They took it out on me.

So I'll take it out on you.

John Foster

Does it make you feel grown-up?

Does it make you feel grown-up

to make the small kids cry?

Can't you see they've had enough,

when tears fall from their eyes?

It isn't big, it isn't brave,

so tell us why you do it.

I'm sure you would not like it much,

if you were going through it.

Richard Caley

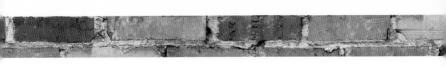

Dad says

Dad says bullies are cowards.

Dad says bullies are sad.

Dad says bullies have tiny minds

and that's what makes them bad.

Dad says I should tell them that

they're cowards and they're sad.

But Dad doesn't go to school with them:

'Swap places with me, Dad!'

Celia Warren

If he hits you

'If he hits you, hit him back.'

That's what my father said.

So I hit him and now I am

in trouble with the Head.

He hit me first. He started it.

I didn't want a fight.

Now I'm in trouble with the Head

and I don't think that's right.

John Foster

Friends?

My friends make fun of Jenny.

I really don't know why.

But they all think they're clever,

if they can make her cry.

They say, 'We're only teasing,'

when I try to stop them.

They say I can't stay in their gang,

if I go and shop them.

Their teasing's really bullying.

And I don't want to hang

around with 'friends' like that, but I'm

afraid to leave their gang.

Celia Warren

If you want to join the gang

They said that I had to do it,

if I wanted to join their gang.

So I waited with them outside the school

when they picked on Tony Chang.

I was there when they jumped on him.

I was there when they ripped his shirt.

I was there when they emptied out his bag

and kicked his books in the dirt.

They said that I had to do it,

if I wanted to join their gang,

but now I feel bad that I was there

when they picked on Tony Chang.

John Foster

29

Don't look at me

Don't look at me like that.

I know I should have stayed.

I should have come to help.

I was afraid.

I saw them rip your books.

I saw them pull your hair.

I wanted to shout 'STOP!'

I didn't dare.

I know I should have stayed.

Not left you on your own.

But I was scared of them,

and I ran home.

Cynthia Rider

Bullies ahead

Cross over.

Head down.

Eyes front.

Mouth shut.

Quick march.

Stay cool.

Keep going.

Straight on.

Get past.

Don't turn.

Never look back.

Hope for the best.

Mike Jubb

Walk tall

'Walk tall,' Dad said. 'Hold up your head.

Don't ever let them see

you're scared.'

But there are four of them

and only one of me.

As I walk past, they turn and stare,

but I don't let them see

I'm scared,

'Cause there are four of them

and only one of me.

John Foster

Eight ways to beat a bully

1 Walk tall.

2 Stay cool.

3 Tell a teacher at school.

4 Tell your friends.

5 Never cry.

6 Hold your head up high.

7 Pretend you don't care.

8 Don't let the bully see you're scared.

Roger Stevens

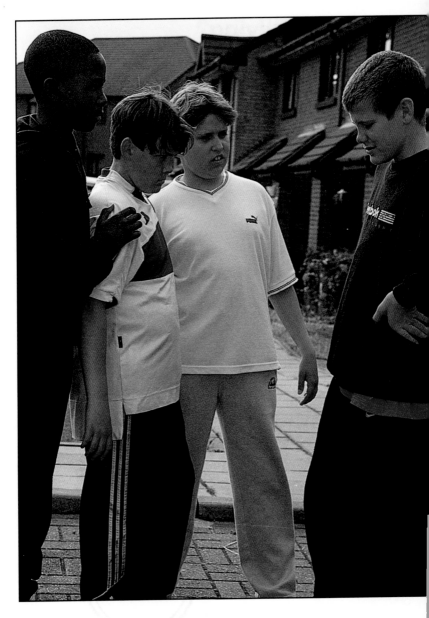

Bullying – the facts

What is bullying?

Lots of people get bullied. Some famous people, including the boxer Frank Bruno and the radio D.J. Janice Long, were bullied when they were young.

There are several different kinds of bullying. Here's what some people said when they were asked: What is bullying?

When people pick on you and call you names

When you're being teased all the time

When people take your things without asking

When people won't speak to you or won't let you join in their games

When people say they'll beat you up, if you don't do what they want

When someone hits or kicks you, or keeps on trying to pick a fight with you

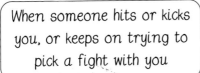

Can you think of any other kinds of bullying?

What does it feel like to be bullied?

Bullies often say they are just having a laugh. But it's not very funny when you're the person who is being bullied. Bullying hurts.

Here are two people describing what they felt when they were bullied.

I thought the whole world was against me. I thought it must be something I'd done. It's stopped now. But it's taken me a long time to start feeling good about myself again.

Jay

Every time I went out they'd shout at me. It got so bad that I stopped going out. I'd sit in my room and cry all the time. Or I'd shut myself in the bathroom. I kept it all bottled up inside. I even thought about running away.

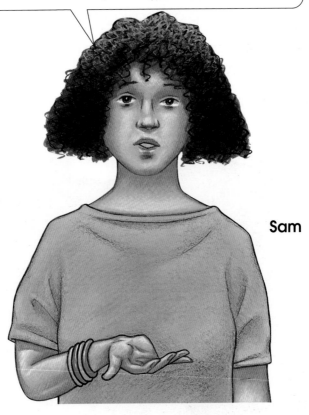

Sam

How would you feel if you were Jay or Sam?

Why do some people get bullied?

People get picked on for all kinds of different reasons. Some people get picked on because they are clever. Others get teased because they aren't clever and they keep on making mistakes.

Often bullies pick on someone who is different from them in some way.

Sometimes bullies pick on a person because they come from a different race. This is called racism.

Why do some people become bullies?

Some people become bullies because they were bullied themselves when they were younger.

Many bullies are unhappy in some way. So they take out their anger on someone else.

But bullying does not help them to sort out their problems. It only causes more problems.

What should you do, if you are bullied?

Some people who are being bullied write letters to problem pages asking for help. Here is a letter that Dave wrote.

ALI'S AGONY COLUMN

Dear Ali

This older boy has started picking on me. He comes and finds me at breaktime. He and his mates take my bag. They throw it about so I can't reach it.

They've started making me give them my dinner money. Now they are saying it's not enough and they want more. What should I do?

Dave

Here is what Ali said in his letter back to Dave.

Dear Dave

Start by telling one of the teachers. Tell your Mum and Dad too. What they are doing to you is more than bullying. They are robbing you of your dinner money.

If they still keep picking on you, tell the teacher again. Keep on telling someone until the bullying stops.

Ali

ALI'S AGONY COLUMN

Ways to beat the bullies

Here is a fact sheet that one school produced to help stop bullying.

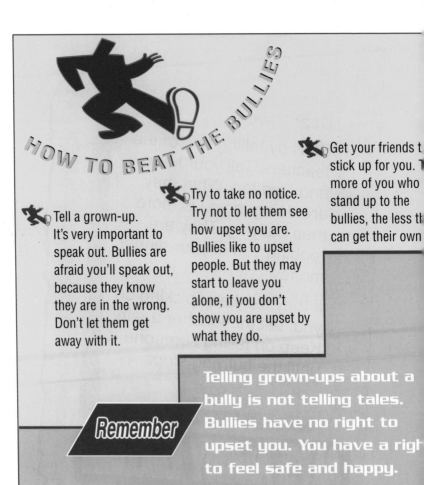

HOW TO BEAT THE BULLIES

Tell a grown-up. It's very important to speak out. Bullies are afraid you'll speak out, because they know they are in the wrong. Don't let them get away with it.

Try to take no notice. Try not to let them see how upset you are. Bullies like to upset people. But they may start to leave you alone, if you don't show you are upset by what they do.

Get your friends t stick up for you. T more of you who stand up to the bullies, the less th can get their own

Remember

Telling grown-ups about a bully is not telling tales. Bullies have no right to upset you. You have a righ to feel safe and happy.

Words to remember

racism
When you treat someone differently because they come from a different race

---

Who can help?

If you are being bullied, there are people you can phone up or write to for help.

You can call these numbers:

Anti-Bullying Campaign
0207 378 1446

ChildLine
(A free, 24-hour helpline for children in trouble or danger)
0800 1111

You can write to:

kidscape

Kidscape
2 Grosvenor Gardens
London SW1W 0DH
or visit their website:
www.kidscape.org.uk/kidscape

Published by HarperCollins *Publishers* Limited
77-85 Fulham Palace Road
Hammersmith
London
W6 8JB

www.**Collins**Education.com
On-line support for schools and colleges

First published 2001

Reprinted 2001

ISBN Stage 2: 0-00-323084-8

British Library Cataloguing in Publication Data
A catalogue record for this publication is available from
the British Library

Acknowledgements
The following permissions to reproduce material are gratefully
acknowledged:

© Bubbles: John Powell, pp5, 33; Frans Rombout, p7; Pauline Cutler,
pp12–13, 14–15, 17, 19, 27, 30–31, 34–35, 37; Angela Hampton, pp8–9;
David Lane, p21; Ian West, pp18, 24; Denise Hager, p25. © Trip/H
Rogers, pp11, 23, 29.

Illustrated by Mike Dodd

Cover design and internal design by Ken Vail Graphic Design, Cambridge

Cover photograph © Bubbles/Denise Hager

Commissioning Editor: Helen Clark

Edited by Lucy Hobbs, John Foster and Rachel Normington

Production: Katie Morris

Printed and bound by
Printing Express, Hong Kong

Get Off My Back!

Poems about bullying